On the Farm

David Elliott
illustrated by Holly Meade

CANDLEWICK PRESS

First paperback edition 2012

The Library of Congress has cataloged the hardcover edition as follows:
Elliott, David (David A.), date.
On the farm / David Elliott ; illustrated by Holly Meade.
p. cm.
ISBN 978-0-7636-3322-6 (hardcover)
1. Domestic animals—Juvenile literature. I. Meade, Holly, ill. II. Title.
SF75.5.E45 2008   636—dc22
2007060857

ISBN 978-0-7636-5591-4 (paperback)

15 16 17 APS 10 9 8 7 6 5 4

Printed in Humen, Dongguan, China

This book was typeset in Columbus Semi Bold.
The illustrations are woodblock prints and watercolor.

Candlewick Press
99 Dover Street
Somerville, Massachusetts 02144

visit us at www.candlewick.com

To Kirsten Cappy and all the kids at Curious City —D. E.

To my neighbor-farmer, young Walker Ellsworth, of Carding Brook Farm —H. M.

The Rooster

Crows and struts.
He's got feathers!
He's got guts!

Oh, the rooster
struts and crows.
What's he thinking?

No one knows.

The Cow

Makes milk
standing
grazing.

Abra-
cada-
bra!

She's
utterly
amazing!

The Pony

Whinnies in the wind.
Kicks in his stall.
He's as mighty as his cousin,
just not as tall.

The Dog

Sleeps
with
one
eye
open
in the shady
farmhouse yard.

You might think
he's keeping cool.
Beware!
He's keeping guard!

The Sheep

Began his woolly life
as gentle as a
lamb. Too bad
he turned
into a
ram.

The Barn Cat

Mice
had better
think twice.

The Goat

Eats everything
from trash to trillium.
Hey! Look out!
He'll knock you silly.
When he's bad,
we call him William.
When he's good,
he's just our Billy.

The Pig

Her tail? As coy as a ringlet.
In her eye there's a delicate sheen.
Some look at her and see a sow;
I see a beauty queen.

The Snake

Coils
   in the
garden
     like a
spring or
     the wild
and winding
     melody
    he
     hears
   but
    cannot
    sing.

The Bees

Tell their story,
sweet and old.
It begins in clover;
it ends with gold.

The Bull

Knows what he likes—
cows and corn.
Knows what he is—
muscle and horn.

The Turtle

Lifts her fossil head
and blinks
one, two, three
times in the awful light.

In her house,
it's always night.

But the Rabbit

Listens.

Listens.   Listens.

And

doesn't

make

a

sound.